★ ★ ★ ★ ★ ★ MILITARY FA

My Mom Is in the
NAVY

NANCY MILLER

PowerKiDS
press.

New York

Published in 2016 by The Rosen Publishing Group, Inc.
29 East 21st Street, New York, NY 10010

First Edition

Editor: Sarah Machajewski
Book Design: Katelyn Heinle/Reann Nye

Photo Credits: Cover, pp. 5, 22 (soldier) Catherine Ledner/The Image Bank/ Getty Images; cover background Markovka/Shutterstock.com; cover backdrop, p. 1 David Smart/Shutterstock.com; pp. 3–4, 6, 8, 10, 12, 14, 16, 18, 20, 22, 24 (camouflage texture) Casper1774/Shutterstock.com; p 7 (top) Maxim Tupikov/ Shutterstock.com; pp. 7 (bottom), 9 (top), 13 (both), 17 (top), 19 (both) courtesy of U.S. Navy Flickr; p. 9 (bottom) lightwavemedia/Shutterstock.com; p. 11 Chris Hondros/Getty Images News/Getty Images; p. 15 Stocktrek Images/ Getty Images; p. 17 (bottom) https://commons.wikimedia.org/wiki/File-Aerial_ view_of_U.S._Naval_Base_Yokosuka,_-26_May_1994_a.jpg; p. 21 John Burke/ Photolibrary/Getty Images; p. 22 (American flag) Naypong/Shutterstock.com; p. 22 (flag background) Naypong/Shutterstock.com.

Library of Congress Cataloging-in-Publication Data

Miller, Nancy, 1964- author.
My mom is in the Navy / Nancy Miller.
    pages cm. — (Military families)
Includes index.
ISBN 978-1-5081-4438-0 (pbk.)
ISBN 978-1-5081-4439-7 (6 pack)
ISBN 978-1-5081-4440-3 (library binding)
1. United States. Navy—Women—Juvenile literature. 2. Women sailors—United States—Juvenile literature. I. Title.
VB324.W65M55 2016
359.0082'0973—dc23
                              2015031619

Manufactured in the United States of America

CPSIA Compliance Information: Batch #BW16PK: For Further Information contact Rosen Publishing, New York, New York at 1-800-237-9932

CONTENTS

MY SPECIAL MOM

My mom has been all over the world. It's not just because she likes to travel—she does it for her job. My mom is a sailor in the U.S. Navy. As a sailor, my mom serves and **protects** the United States. She keeps people like you and me safe.

The navy is just one branch of our country's military. Sailors work on ships in oceans around the world. It's not always easy having a parent in the navy, but I know my mom's job is really important. Let me tell you all about it.

MY MOM'S UNIFORM TELLS THE WORLD SHE'S A PROUD SAILOR IN THE U.S. NAVY.

A Look at the Military

The U.S. military has five branches. The navy is the branch my mom serves in. The other branches are the army, the Marine **Corps**, the coast guard, and the air force. Together, the five branches are known as the "armed forces." They work together to **defend** the United States in the air, on land, and at sea.

The navy is one of the largest military branches. It's a water-based force, which means sailors such as my mom fight at sea. Sailors serve on ships, including battleships, **destroyers**, submarines, and even special kinds of aircraft.

★ ★ ★

MILITARY MATTERS

The navy and Marine Corps belong to the Department of the Navy.

ALL BRANCHES OF THE MILITARY WORK TOGETHER, BUT THE U.S. NAVY WORKS THE MOST WITH THE MARINE CORPS AND THE COAST GUARD. ALL THREE OF THESE BRANCHES WORK AT SEA.

Naval History

The U.S. Navy has been around for a long time. It's 240 years old! It was formed on October 13, 1775. During the American Revolution, colonial leaders felt a navy was needed to protect the colonies against powerful British warships. The Continental navy was formed to do just that, but it didn't last after the war.

The U.S. Navy formed again in 1794. Since then, this important branch has grown to have more than 400,000 sailors. Most sailors work for the navy full time. Some sailors are part of the Navy Reserve, which means they work for the navy part time.

★★★
Military Matters
Before the Continental navy formed, some colonies, including Rhode Island and Massachusetts, had their own navy.

ACTIVE-DUTY
SAILOR

NAVY RESERVE
SAILOR

ACTIVE-DUTY SAILORS SUCH AS MY MOM WORK FOR THE NAVY FULL TIME. NAVY RESERVE SAILORS HAVE REGULAR JOBS BUT SERVE WHEN THE COUNTRY NEEDS THEM.

BECOMING A SAILOR

My mom **enlisted** in the navy before I was born. Every sailor that enlists has to meet certain requirements. First, sailors have to be between 18 and 34 years old. In general, sailors have to be U.S. citizens, but people from other countries who have lawfully entered the United States are allowed to enlist, too.

To join the navy, sailors must have completed high school or earned a GED, which is much like having a high school education. The navy also makes sure all of its sailors have a good **background**. It may not accept people who have been in trouble with the law.

SAILORS USUALLY TALK TO A RECRUITER BEFORE ENLISTING. A RECRUITER WORKS WITH SAILORS AND THEIR FAMILIES TO SEE IF JOINING THE NAVY IS RIGHT FOR THEM. IT'S A BIG DECISION, AND RECRUITERS CAN MAKE IT EASIER.

★★★
MILITARY MATTERS
To enlist in the navy at 17, you need special permission from your parents.

GOING TO BOOT CAMP

After signing up, my mom took a test called the ASVAB. This test helps sailors figure out what career they'll have with the navy. Then, she took the **Oath** of Enlistment. She was officially a sailor!

After my mom enlisted, she went to Recruit Training in Great Lakes, Illinois. It's sometimes called boot camp. Boot camp lasts between seven and nine weeks. During training, sailors learn the skills they need to serve in the navy. They learn about naval ships and how to fight when they're on board. They also learn how to work together and solve problems.

IT CAN BE HARD WHEN A SAILOR GOES AWAY FOR TRAINING. THEY'RE GONE FOR ABOUT TWO MONTHS, AND YOU CAN'T TALK TO THEM OFTEN. MY DAD SAID HE MISSED MY MOM WHEN SHE WAS AWAY.

TRAINING TO DIVE

After boot camp, my mom went through two more kinds of training. They're called "A" School and "C" School. There are schools for officers and other specialized jobs, too. In all these schools, sailors learn the skills needed for their career in the navy.

My mom is navy diver. Navy divers go on **assignments** deep in the ocean. They perform search-and-rescue missions. They also look after and help fix navy ships. This is a really hard job. This isn't the only navy career, though. Sailors can be **engineers**, lawyers, doctors, **meteorologists**, and more.

NAVY DIVERS HAVE TO BE GREAT SWIMMERS—MOST OF THEIR JOB TAKES PLACE IN THE WATER!

LIFE ON A NAVAL BASE

My mom's job affects my family's life. It determines where we live. I was born in New York. When I was young, the navy gave my mom a job in another state, which meant we had to move. We moved to Hawaii! We might have to move again in the future.

My family lives on a naval base. A naval base is where sailors train and equipment is held. All our neighbors also have a family member in the navy. My friends and I go to school in the town closest to the navy base. My home is probably a lot like yours.

★★★
MILITARY MATTERS
The United States has naval bases all over the world, including in other countries. They're often near oceans!

MY MOM WORKS ON A SHIP THAT'S DOCKED AT THE NAVAL BASE. THE SHIPS ARE REALLY BIG AND REALLY COOL, TOO!

Away at Sea

My mom's job is a lot like a regular job. She goes to work in the morning and picks us up from school. We make dinner together and watch movies. However, sometimes she gets sent out on a mission at sea. This is called deployment.

Navy families know that deployment is hard. My mom can be at sea for six months at a time. I miss my mom a lot when she's deployed, and I know she misses me, too. I feel better when I write her letters or talk to her on the phone.

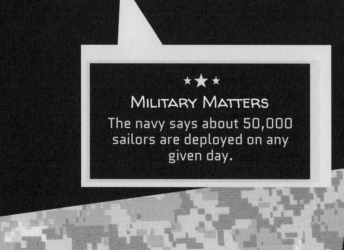

★ ★ ★
Military Matters
The navy says about 50,000 sailors are deployed on any given day.

WHEN MY MOM IS DEPLOYED, SHE LIVES AND WORKS ON A SHIP. SHE AND OTHER SAILORS SPEND A LOT OF TIME ON THE MESS DECK. THAT'S WHERE THEY EAT AND RELAX.

THE REAL DEAL

I feel really happy when my mom comes home from being deployed. My dad and I count down the days on a calendar! The last time she came home, we made her a welcome home sign. She was happy, too.

A lot of people wonder what it's like to have a parent in the navy. I think it makes my family very special. We love each other very much, and we're proud of my mom's job. She always keeps my family safe, but when she's serving at sea, she keeps our whole country safe, too.

SAILORS NEED THEIR FAMILY'S SUPPORT, ESPECIALLY WHEN THEY'RE SERVING AWAY FROM HOME.

My Hero

If you don't have a family member in the military, you might wonder what it's like. The best way to learn is to ask someone who does. Military families are proud of their soldier or sailor. I know I'm very proud of my mom.

My mom's job isn't easy. She's always training so she can keep her skills and knowledge up to date. She has to leave my family when she deploys. But she knows that these **sacrifices** are worth it. She's a sailor for the U.S. Navy, and she's my hero.

Glossary

active duty: Having to do with full-time service in the military. Also, full-time service in the military.

assignment: A task given to someone.

background: A person's life experiences.

corps: A group within a branch of a military organization that does a particular kind of work.

defend: To keep safe from harm or danger.

destroyer: A small, fast warship.

engineer: A person who designs, builds, or cares for engines and machines.

enlist: To join.

meteorologist: Someone who predicts the weather.

oath: An official promise.

protect: To keep safe.

sacrifice: Something given up for a larger purpose.

INDEX

WEBSITES

Due to the changing nature of Internet links, PowerKids Press has developed an online list of websites related to the subject of this book. This site is updated regularly. Please use this link to access the list: www.powerkidslinks.com/mili/navy